KEE

CW01509232

HODGKINSON

The

Heart of a Champion, The Drive for Gold, and The Spirit of an Athlete

Bravo J. Max

Copyright © 2024 by Bravo J. Max

All rights reserved.

No part of this publication may be reproduced, distributed, or transmitted in any form or by any means, including photocopying or other electronic or mechanical methods, without the prior written permission of the publisher, except in the case of brief quotations embodied in reviews and certain other non-commercial uses permitted by copyright law.

Cover Image Credit;

The cover image File: Keely Hodgkinson at 2023 European Indoor Championships2.jpg

Author: Erik van Leeuwen, attribution: Erik van Leeuwen (bron: Wikipedia).

Licensed under the Creative Commons Attribution-Share Alike 4.0 international license

Source:

https://erki.zenfolio.com/p611090201/h5b0226a1#h 5b0226a1

DISCLAIMER

This book is an independent biography about Keely Hodgkinson, celebrating her athletic career and personal journey. It is based on publicly available information, interviews, and the author's interpretations. While every effort has been made to provide accurate information, this book is not endorsed by Keely Hodgkinson or any official representatives. It does not claim to have exclusive rights or insider details about her private life or future endeavors. All opinions and interpretations are solely those of the author, intended for educational and inspirational purposes. Readers are encouraged to verify any information that may be subject to change over time.

TABLE OF CONTENTS

INTRODUCTION

Athlete Keely Hodgkinson's incredible ascent to the top of her field is evidence of her champion mentality, unmatched determination, and resiliency. Keely, who was born in 2002 in Atherton, Greater Manchester, started running when she was nine years old and showed early promise that would propel her to stardom. However, few could have guessed exactly how swiftly she would soar, becoming one of the most recognized faces in middle-distance racing by the age of 22.

At the 2020 Tokyo Olympics, a 19-year-old Hodgkinson astonished the world by clinching a silver medal in the 800 meters, breaking the long-standing British record previously set by Kelly Holmes. In that moment, it became evident that Keely was not simply a rising star but a force to be reckoned with. Ever since then, she has been hell-bent on winning the gold medal at the 2024 Paris Olympics, and her dogged persistence paid off. Running a planned race in the women's 800m final, Keely led from the front and withstood a tough push from competitors like Ethiopia's Tsige Duguma and Kenya's Mary Moraa, ultimately crossing the finish line in a scorching 1:56.72 to earn her maiden Olympic gold medal.

These three periods in Keely's career—"The Heart of a Champion, The Drive for Gold, and The Spirit of an Athlete"—serve as inspiration for the book's title. It portrays her track talent as well as her tenacity and dedication, which have brought her to the top of her discipline. Each word in the title highlights a vital part of her journey: the heart that beats with determination, the drive that pushes her past every hurdle, and the spirit that remains unbroken in the face of failures.

Motivation: The Unceasing Quest for Greatness

The path to success for Keely Hodgkinson has been fraught with difficulty. Hurts, self-doubt, and intense rivalry are common experiences for great athletes. Injury setbacks plagued Keely in 2023, causing her to miss multiple weeks of training owing to problems with her knee and hamstring ligaments and tendons. Still, her remarkable mental resilience is on full display in how she recovers from setbacks. By working closely with medical specialists and focusing on recuperation, Keely proved once again that her drive to succeed has no limitations.

This drive was particularly visible in her preparation for the 2024 Paris Olympics. Despite the great pressure of being the favorite, Keely kept her focus and composure, building on her already remarkable accomplishments in major championships like the World Championships and the European Championships. Her silver medals in Tokyo (2021), Eugene (2022), and Budapest (2023) were stepping stones on the route to her ultimate goal—Olympic gold.

Spirit: Rising Above Challenges

Keely's journey has been distinguished not simply by wins but by the hurdles she has had to face. From injuries to difficult opponents, she has never taken the easy road. Her rivalry with Athing Mu of the United States and Mary Moraa of Kenya has marked some of her greatest races. At the 2023 World Championships in Budapest, for example, Hodgkinson finished close behind Moraa, just missing out on the gold. But instead of wiping away defeat, she used it as fuel, learning from each race and coming back stronger.

Her spirit has also shined through in how she handles pressure. Reflecting on her victory in Paris, Keely observed, "I've worked so hard for this," praising not just her own effort but the support of her team and fans. Her ability to stay collected under duress, as she did when she saw Moraa coming in on her in the last stretch, highlights the mental power that has become a trademark of her career.

Heart: The Champion's Mindset

Perhaps the most defining attribute of Keely Hodgkinson is her heart—the enthusiasm she takes to every race and the dedication she pours into her preparation. From a young age, Keely has demonstrated a tenacious work ethic, continually pushing the boundaries of what she can achieve. Even in the face of setbacks, she has shown an extraordinary capacity for self-belief and perseverance, attributes that make her an inspiring figure both on and off the track.

Her victory in Paris not only crowned her an Olympic champion but also secured her standing as a role model for future generations of athletes. As Keely herself observed, "The future is bright," a message that connects emotionally with those who follow her work. Her enthusiasm for the sport, mixed with her modesty and grounded character, makes her a unique presence in the world of athletics.

In the chapters that follow, this book will cover Keely Hodgkinson's extraordinary journey from her early days in Atherton to standing atop the podium at the Paris Olympics. We will go deep into the races, rivalries, and tireless quest for greatness that characterizes her. But more significantly, we will find the heart, determination, and passion that have made Keely Hodgkinson a true champion and an inspiration to everyone who aspires to reach the highest heights of accomplishment.

CHAPTER 1

THE EARLY STRIDES OF A CHAMPION

1.1: Beginnings

Keely Hodgkinson's journey into the world of athletics is a narrative distinguished by youthful ambition, dedication, and a family with profound respect for sports. Born on March 3, 2002, in Atherton, Greater Manchester, Hodgkinson grew up in an environment that celebrated physical activity. Her father, Dean, was a former rugby player and marathon runner, and her mother, Rachel, also had a career in athletics. This impact established the groundwork for Keely's early interest in sports. She originally investigated swimming, joining the Howe Bridge Aces swim club, but soon found her true passion in running, aged nine, when she joined

Leigh Harriers & Athletic Club. From then on, her journey in track and field began to take form.

One of Keely's earliest inspirations came from witnessing British heptathlete Jessica Ennis-Hill earn gold at the 2012 London Olympics. For the young Keely, Ennis-Hill's accomplishment generated a sense of possibility and set the bar for what she could achieve in her own athletic career. Reflecting on these early influences, Keely has often spoken about the importance of watching competitors like Ennis-Hill in her dreams, fueling a drive for competitiveness that would carry her through the ups and downs of her early training years.

In her formative years, Keely's skill became clear to coaches and competitors alike. She originally made her mark at the age of 10, competing in the British Schools Modern Biathlon Championships. Her performance in the 500-meter race earned her a personal best and helped her position in the top 10 overall, identifying her as a bright young athlete in British track and field. Soon after, Keely began winning local events, distinguishing herself as an emerging star. By the age of 13, she had already achieved trophies in cross-country and track sports, including double wins in Greater Manchester championships in both the 800 and 1200 meters.

Her early years were not without problems. In 2015, aged just 13, Keely had a medical setback after undergoing mastoidectomy surgery, which left her with partial hearing loss in one ear. Despite this, her enthusiasm for running remained undaunted. She handled her condition while maintaining her training and continued to chase success on the track. Her resilience through this period illustrates a significant element in her life—the ability to adapt and overcome adversities, something that would prove vital as she moved into more competitive areas.

Keely's breakout continued into her mid-teens, when she began competing at national and international levels. In 2018, at just 16, she took her first national gold in the 800 meters at the England Athletics U20 Championships, recording a personal best. Shortly after, she prevailed at the European U18 Championships in Győr, Hungary, with a gold medal performance that showcased her growth and commitment. By then, her outstanding talent and ferocious competitive spirit were clear, confirming her status as one of Britain's most promising middle-distance runners.

Looking back, Keely's early years created a foundation not only of athletic prowess but of resilience and mental toughness. She recalls her earlier races fondly, sharing how those events taught her crucial lessons in tenacity. Reflecting on her journey, she has acknowledged her family and coaches for developing her enthusiasm and ambition, highlighting that her formative circumstances were essential in molding her profession. This period in her life marked the beginning of an extraordinary athletic journey, one driven by her innate "heart of a champion." Her remarkable ascent from a young runner inspired by Olympic legends to one of Britain's top middle-distance competitors is a testament to her relentless pursuit of excellence from a young age.

This blend of family influence, inspiration from sporting heroes, and early triumphs in competitive circumstances formed a foundation upon which Keely would build her future successes. Her tale from early beginnings embodies the elements of heart, passion, and spirit that define her path as an elite athlete.

1.2: The Foundation of Dedication

Keely Hodgkinson's path in athletics has been distinguished by determination, persistence, and a sequence of triumphs that created the framework for her career. Starting with modest, local events, she swiftly acquired a reputation as an athlete with outstanding skill and a tenacious work ethic, hitting big milestones in young championships across the UK and Europe.

Keely's competitive path began to gain speed when, at just 10 years old, she started making waves in regional races with Leigh Harriers & Athletic Club, where she trained under the tutelage of experienced coaches who recognised her raw ability. One of her earlier successes came at the British Schools Modern Biathlon Championships. Competing among the greatest young athletes from across the nation, Keely's second-place finish in the 500 meters announced her debut as a formidable talent in junior athletics. Her regular performances in cross-country and track competitions, even at this young age, showed her innate knack for running and her commitment to greatness.

The years that followed saw her capture a series of age-group titles, confirming her reputation as one of

Britain's most promising middle-distance runners. In the early phases of her career, Keely exhibited not only her speed but also her mental resilience, displaying a level of attention and determination rare in young athletes. Her father, Dean Hodgkinson, has commented on Keely's work ethic, saying, "She's always been incredibly disciplined and focused, even from a young age. Her drive has been the key to her success."

In 2018, Keely claimed her first national title in the England Athletics U20 Championships in the 800 meters, achieving a personal best time that highlighted her growth as an athlete. That year marked a critical stage in her career, as she went on to represent Great Britain at the European U18 Championships in Győr, Hungary. In the 800-meter final, Keely executed a well-planned racing strategy, positioning herself at the front early on before storming ahead in the final stretch. Her gold medal triumph at Győr was a milestone achievement, cementing her standing as a top prospect in British athletics and setting her on a trajectory toward elite contests. Speaking about that accomplishment, Keely reminisced, "Winning in Győr was a dream come true. It made all the hard work worth it and showed me what was possible if I kept pushing myself."

Beyond her triumphs, Keely's formative years in athletics were defined by a series of trials that only appeared to increase her resolve. In 2015, she encountered a big challenge when she underwent surgery, which resulted in partial hearing loss. Despite the setback, Keely returned to the track with a newfound feeling of drive, embracing her hurdles as part of her journey rather than obstacles to her accomplishment. She continued to train consistently, reconciling her scholastic commitments with her athletic objectives, an achievement that garnered her the respect of her coaches and classmates.

As Keely's success in youth events persisted, she began to gain the attention of the greater sports world. In 2019, her exploits in the English Schools' Championships and other national tournaments further established her as an athlete with the ability to make a difference on the global scene. At the England U17 Championships, she ran a spectacular performance, setting a new personal best and further lowering her time in the 800 meters. Her progress that season culminated in a sequence of remarkable finishes, each race a step ahead in her pursuit of excellence.

Her coach, Trevor Painter, who has played a vital role in her growth, remarked on her ability to focus and execute race strategies with maturity beyond her years. Painter observed, "Keely's mindset has always been her strength. She tackles each race with a definite strategy, and she knows how to handle pressure. That's what sets her apart." Painter's guidance, along with Keely's own discipline, has been instrumental in shaping her competitive edge.

Keely's victories in young contests were not only the result of natural talent; they were the outcome of numerous hours of focused training, mental preparation, and a passion to succeed that was clear to anybody who saw her race. Her performances throughout these years created the framework for her success on the senior circuit and gave her the experience needed to excel at the highest levels of competition. By the time she went onto the track for her debut in major international competitions, Keely had already polished the talents and mental toughness that would become characteristics of her career.

Reflecting on these early events, Keely has attributed her youth competitions with teaching her essential lessons in resilience and discipline. Her journey through the ranks of British junior athletics not only molded her into a champion but also established a strong appreciation for the sport. In her own words, "Every race, every competition taught me something important. It was never just about winning; it was about learning and growing better."

These formative years, defined by wins and losses alike, established the basis upon which Keely would build her career, exhibiting the attributes that distinguish a champion: resilience, devotion, and an unshakeable drive to be the greatest.

1.3: Rising Through the Ranks

Keely Hodgkinson's entrance into professional sports began with a string of outstanding performances, highlighted with a decisive moment in 2021 that took her to the global stage. While she had already made a name for herself at the youth level, it was her record-breaking performances and coolness under pressure that placed her on a course toward becoming one of the most promising middle-distance runners in the world.

Keely's ascension began to quicken at the 2018 European U18 Championships in Győr, Hungary, when she earned the gold in the 800 meters. This triumph was followed by a bronze medal at the 2019 European U20 Championships in Borås, Sweden, highlighting her consistency at the international level and establishing her as a significant player in British athletics. The success in these competitions underlined her innate tactical understanding and the physical endurance that would come to define her racing style as she matured.

In early 2021, Keely accomplished a historic step by being the youngest British athlete in more than half a century to win a European Indoor Championship. Just days after turning 19, she participated in Torun, Poland, where she dominated the 800 meters with a time of 2:03.88, leaping past seasoned competitors like Poland's Joanna Jozwik and Angelika Cichocka. Her triumph was not only a personal milestone but also a symbolic passing of the torch; her coach, Trevor Painter, and mentor Jenny Meadows—who won the same title a decade earlier—played a vital part in her growth. This win launched Keely on a clear road toward elite-level competition and gave her the confidence to compete with the best in the world.

Hodgkinson's achievement in Torun placed her firmly on the radar of British Athletics, and she set her sights on an even wider stage: the Tokyo Olympics. The preparation for Tokyo took an unparalleled amount of attention and resilience from Keely, especially in a year challenged by the COVID-19 epidemic. She worked closely with her trainers, who ensured that her training was adaptable and comprehensive, helping her refine her physical and mental skills in ways that would prepare her for the stresses of the Olympic stage.

The Tokyo Olympics would be Keely's professional breakout in every sense. She began the games as an underdog in the 800 meters, facing stiff opposition from American favorites Athing Mu and other top-tier runners. However, Keely ran an excellent race, finishing in 1:55.88—a new British record—earning the silver medal and making her the youngest British woman to secure a podium finish in track and field at the Olympics. Breaking the national record set by the famous Kelly Holmes in 1995, Keely's performance enthralled viewers across the world and signified the advent of a new era in British middle-distance running.

Reflecting on her Tokyo performance, Keely observed, "It still hasn't sunk in. Breaking the British record and getting silver was beyond my expectations. I wanted to make my country and my family proud, and I think I did that." Her dad, Dean Hodgkinson, expressed the pride of her family: "We knew she could get there. It's fantastic to watch all she's worked for become reality."

Keely's silver medal in Tokyo signified not only a personal achievement but also a watershed moment for British sports. Following Tokyo, she continued her extraordinary momentum with silver medals at the World Championships in Eugene in 2022 and in Budapest in 2023, indicating that her performance in Tokyo was no fluke. Keely's consistency and poise in high-stakes contests have confirmed her standing as one of Britain's most promising athletes and an emerging icon in middle-distance running.

The route that led Keely Hodgkinson to professional athletics demonstrates a mix of talent, determination, and the unshakeable belief instilled by her family and coaches. Her performance on the global arena reveals a competitive spirit and maturity beyond her years, and her historic feats in Tokyo and beyond serve as an inspiration for young athletes worldwide.

CHAPTER 2

CHASING GOLD

2.1: Tokyo 2020

Keely Hodgkinson's journey at the Tokyo 2020 Olympics was nothing short of remarkable. At just 19, she entered the Games relatively unknown on the global scene but left as a rising star in British sports. Her achievement—winning a silver medal in the 800 meters and breaking a long-standing British record—signaled a new beginning in her career and revived middle-distance running in the UK.

Leading up to Tokyo, Keely had already shown remarkable promise. In January 2021, she clocked 1:59.03 at an indoor event in Vienna, making her the fastest under-20 woman in the 800 meters for that year. The following month, she became the youngest British woman to win a European Indoor

Championship in over fifty years, capturing gold in the 800 meters in Torun, Poland. These victories laid the basis for her Olympic debut and inspired her drive to participate on the world's biggest sports platform.

In the 800-meter final in Tokyo, Keely faced a competition stacked with top-tier talent, including American sensation Athing Mu, who had rapidly become the favorite for gold. Keely positioned herself intelligently during the race, hanging back in the pack yet conserving energy. With 300 meters to go, she produced a tremendous kick, moving from fifth place to capture the silver medal with a timing of 1:55.88. This amazing effort not only earned her a position on the podium but also surpassed the British record set by Kelly Holmes in 1995, a record that had been held for 26 years.

Reflecting on the race, Keely told the BBC, "It was so open, and I wanted to put it all out there; I'm so happy." Her victory was particularly meaningful, as she looked up to Holmes as a childhood hero. This performance marked Team GB's first track and field medal at the Tokyo Games and captured the attention of fans around the world. It also made her the fourth-fastest under-20 runner in the 800 meters in history, cementing her place among the world's elite in middle-distance running.

Keely's journey to silver in Tokyo resonated deeply back home, especially given the challenges she had faced in getting there. Due to the COVID-19 pandemic, she had not been added to British Athletics' World Class Performance Program in 2020, meaning she had to work with limited resources compared to some of her competitors. Supported by her mentor Jenny Meadows and coach Trevor Painter, Keely trained rigorously, adapting her regimen to ensure she remained competitive. Her determination to succeed, despite these obstacles, underscored the resilience that would define her Olympic journey.

In the wake of her silver medal win, the British public and media hailed Keely as an inspiration, calling her the new face of British athletics. For Keely, this moment was the realization of years of dedication, but it also signaled a fresh start to her professional career, opening up new possibilities on the international stage. Her Tokyo performance not only redefined her personal career trajectory but also contributed to a larger revival of excitement for middle-distance events in the UK.

The Tokyo Olympics proved to be more than simply a race for Keely; it was a turning point that established her capacity to compete with the best and set the path for future dreams, including her pursuit of gold in future World Championships and Olympic Games.

2.2: Lessons from Tokyo

Keely Hodgkinson's experience at the Tokyo 2020 Olympics became a pivotal moment in her career, not just for her remarkable performance but for the lessons she took away from the high-pressure environment of the Games. Reflecting on her silver medal, which she earned with a time of 1:55.88 in the 800 meters, Keely learned essential lessons about resilience, confidence, and handling global competition at such a young age.

One of Keely's key takeaways from Tokyo was learning to maintain focus amidst intense expectations. Entering the Olympics as a 19-year-old relatively new to the senior international stage, she felt a mix of excitement and pressure. She had already broken records and demonstrated talent, yet stepping onto the Olympic track was a significant leap in terms of visibility and competition. Reflecting on this experience, Keely later shared that managing her nerves and staying focused were crucial. In a post-race interview, she acknowledged, "I'm going to carry on doing it. If you don't enjoy it, everything becomes pressured and hard work. As long as I keep doing what I'm doing and stay injury-free, hopefully, there will be many more moments like this.".

The race itself taught her the importance of adaptability and timing. Positioned fifth for much of the race, she made a strategic move in the final 300 meters to secure silver, an approach she attributed to the trust she placed in her training and instincts. Her coach, Trevor Painter, had prepared her to pace effectively, allowing her to unleash her final push precisely when it counted most. Competing against Athing Mu, a similarly young talent and gold medallist, reinforced for Keely the competitive level she aspired to and the importance of learning from rivals to elevate her own performance.

Breaking Kelly Holmes' British record during the race was another significant milestone, both for Keely and for British athletics. She described the achievement as "unbelievable," crediting Holmes as a lifelong inspiration. After receiving supportive messages from Holmes leading up to the event,

Keely expressed both humility and pride, saying that her time in Tokyo was "just the beginning" of what she wanted to achieve.

Beyond athletic insights, the Tokyo experience underscored the importance of a strong support network. Despite not being part of British Athletics' World Class Performance Program due to pandemic restrictions, she received support from her family, coach, and Barrie Wells, a philanthropist who funded her training. This experience taught her the value of staying grounded, as she said, "I just wanted to go on this track and execute. This is what I want to do: be one of the best in the world." She credits her mother's support as a key factor in her growth, helping her navigate the challenges and new pressures that came with her success.

Ultimately, Tokyo was a learning experience that highlighted her readiness for the global stage and motivated her to aim even higher. The confidence gained from Tokyo would propel her toward future championships, transforming a silver medal into a foundation for ongoing growth. She left Tokyo not only with the pride of a medalist, but also with a deeper understanding of her capabilities and the knowledge that her journey was just beginning.

2.3: Building Momentum for Paris 2024

Keely Hodgkinson's path to the Paris 2024 Olympics is a story of calculated growth, physical intensity, and mental strength honed over years since her silver-winning performance in Tokyo 2020. After finishing second to Athing Mu in Tokyo, Hodgkinson emerged as a strong contender for gold, committing to a strategic training plan aimed at achieving that goal.

Central to Hodgkinson's preparation has been her work with her coaches, Trevor Painter and Jenny Meadows, who balance rigorous training with an approach that allows her to stay relaxed and focused. Recognising that Keely thrives under a supportive, flexible structure, Painter and Meadows have built an environment at the M11 Track Club that combines discipline with personal freedom, allowing her to maintain her "free-spirited" style. This environment fosters an approach where Keely races "without a care in the world," something her coaches believe is critical for her best performance under high-pressure conditions.

In physical training, Hodgkinson focused on strengthening her speed, as this would give her an advantage in a competitive field. To improve her explosive pace, she frequently ran 400-meter races, testing her limits and refining her acceleration. Her hard work paid off when she set a new British record of 1:54.61 at the London Diamond League just before the Paris Games. This time was faster than the Tokyo 2020 gold medal mark, and while it provided a confidence boost, Hodgkinson chose to remain focused on the bigger picture, approaching each race in Paris as its own unique challenge.

Altitude training also played a significant role in her buildup to Paris. She attended rigorous altitude camps in locations like the Pyrenees and South Africa to enhance her endurance and lung capacity, further preparing her for the sustained demands of Olympic competition. Painter believes that Hodgkinson has yet to reach her peak, suggesting that her disciplined, long-term preparation could position her as a serious challenger for even the 800m world record in the future.

Mentally, Keely emphasized learning to navigate the complex emotions of being a favorite for gold. Reflecting on her journey, she highlighted that success at this level is as much about mental resilience as it is about physical ability. Rather than focusing on her time alone, she set her sights on executing a race she would be "really happy with," trusting that this focus would lead to a winning performance.

Hodgkinson's journey to Paris reflects an athlete committed not only to her physical training but to cultivating a mindset that allows her to handle the pressure of high-stakes races. Entering the 2024 Olympics as a favorite, Keely's preparation underscores a drive to not just win gold but to redefine her sport through a commitment to both speed and mental fortitude. Her disciplined yet flexible approach, supported by a dedicated team, positioned her to achieve her Paris dreams and set the stage for a legacy in British middle-distance running.

CHAPTER 3

THE SPIRIT OF COMPETITION

3.1: European Championships 2022

At the European Athletics Championships in Munich in 2022, Keely Hodgkinson claimed her first outdoor 800-meter gold medal, a victory that highlighted a year filled with near-wins and marked a new landmark in her career. Her climb to the top in Munich was not merely a display of skill but also one of resilience, considering her back-to-back silvers in earlier contests, including the Tokyo Olympics in 2021, the 2022 World Championships, and the Commonwealth Games held just weeks prior. The Munich tournament brought Hodgkinson's intense resolve to the fore, showcasing her ability to fight through adversities and ultimately secure the top spot.

In the 800-meter final, Hodgkinson's approach was defined by patience and strategy. As the race progressed, she maintained a guarded pace in the early lap, allowing Germany's Christina Hering to establish a quick 400-meter pace of roughly 58.6 seconds. Hodgkinson intentionally took a conservative stance early in the race, waiting to make her decisive move. In the last 200 meters, she pulled away from the group, calling on her reserve strength and power to push ahead. This move consolidated her authority over the race, putting clear distance between herself and competitors such as France's Rénelle Lamote, who grabbed silver with a time of 1:59.49, and Poland's Anna Wielgosz, who took bronze at 1:59.87. Hodgkinson's winning time of 1:59.04 emphasized her competitive prowess and demonstrated her progress in strategic racing and finishing power.

Reflecting on the win, Hodgkinson acknowledged the psychological and physical demands of competing at such a high level across three major tournaments in less than a month. "I think it's more of a mental thing coming into this being my third championship in four and a half weeks," she commented, pointing to the tremendous toll these intensive competitions took on her energy and mindset. Yet she remained resolute in her ambition, claiming, "I refused to walk away today without gold." This toughness, combined with her disciplined approach to racing, highlighted her readiness to overcome hurdles and her commitment to excel on the European arena.

The triumph in Munich also signaled a turning point in Hodgkinson's narrative as a competitor. For months, she had been on the edge of earning major honors, with silver finishes trailing close behind the reigning winners in the field, including Athing Mu from the U.S. at the Olympics and Mary Moraa from Kenya at the Commonwealth Games. Her success in Munich was, therefore, not just a career milestone but also a validation of her potential to dominate in future major tournaments. This win placed Hodgkinson among the best European athletes in middle-distance running and cemented her as a frontrunner in the 800 meters.

Looking at the broader impact, Hodgkinson's triumph generated admiration across the athletic world, as she became a recognized emblem of resilience and unrelenting determination. After the sequence of silvers, many questioned how she would respond; in Munich, she demonstrated that her concentration remained firmly on the gold. In the days after, the European Athletics community praised her accomplishment, hailing her win as the start of a new chapter for British middle-distance running. As she turned her thoughts to future contests, including the highly anticipated Paris Olympics in 2024, her Munich success showed a peek of her talent to execute and win at the greatest level.

Hodgkinson's achievement at the 2022 European Championships not only showcased her athletic ability but also reflected the spirit of determination and the strength required to overcome obstacles. Her journey emphasized a crucial message about resilience in the face of recurrent adversity, placing her not only as a superb athlete but also as a source of inspiration. As she continues her route toward future championships, Hodgkinson's narrative from Munich will likely remain a critical event that displays her progress, tenacity, and unyielding determination to succeed.

3.2: World Championships

At the 2022 World Athletics Championships held in Eugene, Oregon, Keely Hodgkinson faced battle against some of the most formidable athletes in middle-distance running, including her well-matched adversary Athing Mu from the U.S., the reigning Olympic champion. The women's 800-meter final, which took place in July, was an exhibition of tactical prowess and raw competitive passion. Hodgkinson's silver medal was not simply a testimonial to her skill but also her resilience and ability to execute under enormous pressure.

In the race, Mu, known for her aggressive front-running style, originally kept just behind Ethiopia's Diribe Welteji, who claimed the lead in the first 200 meters with Hodgkinson right at Mu's shoulder. Welteji led the field over a quick 400 meters at 57.09 seconds, with Mu and Hodgkinson closely trailing. When Mu made her move around the back stretch, Hodgkinson replied, staying tightly on Mu's inside channel. By the 600-meter mark, the top contenders—Mu, Hodgkinson, and Kenya's Mary Moraa—were comfortably within striking distance of each other. In the final 100 meters, Hodgkinson spotted her opportunity and sprinted forward, briefly coming even with Mu, exhibiting her incredible speed and competitive determination.

Hodgkinson set a season-best time of 1:56.38, barely 0.08 seconds behind Mu, who finished with a world-leading time of 1:56.30. Moraa completed the podium in 1:56.71, achieving a personal best and marking Kenya's first medal in the women's 800 meters at a world championship since 2015. This tight margin between Hodgkinson and Mu revealed the razor-thin gap in ability between these two young competitors, both of whom had previously medaled at the Tokyo Olympics in 2021. Hodgkinson's performance in Eugene emphasized her readiness to fight Mu at every step, and it became evident that her plan and discipline in pacing allowed her to stay close throughout the race.

Reflecting on the race, Hodgkinson recounted her drive to capture the gold, expressing a mix of pride and anger at how close she had come to attaining it. "I thought I could get her in the last 100," she said, noting how she gave it her all but fell just short of Mu's relentless sprint finish. For Hodgkinson, each stride in this race underscored her unyielding resolve to reach the top of the podium—a goal she had narrowly missed on multiple global stages but continued to pursue with tenacity and skill.

This silver medal performance marked a significant chapter in Hodgkinson's career. It was her second world silver in two years, following her Olympic silver in Tokyo, where she also finished close behind Mu. These results solidified Hodgkinson's reputation as one of the world's leading 800-meter runners and hinted at an ongoing rivalry with Mu that would captivate the athletics world. Her determination to keep closing the gap with Mu highlighted her potential to capture global gold in future competitions, setting high expectations as she looked ahead to the upcoming Paris Olympics.

In the broader context of her 2022 season, Hodgkinson's achievements were exceptional. Her performances at each major championship demonstrated not only her consistency but also her adaptability. Competing against world-class athletes across different continents and conditions,

Hodgkinson proved her resilience and mental toughness. Her continued improvement in race times and split-second finishes against the best in the world have established her as a respected competitor and an inspiration within British and global athletics.

As the field looks forward to upcoming championships, Hodgkinson's experiences in Eugene—and her ever-narrowing time gap with Mu—position her as a fierce contender for future titles. For fans and fellow athletes, her journey serves as an inspiring narrative of grit and unwavering commitment to excellence, a testament to the spirit of competition that defines her path in the sport.

3.3: Continental Success

Keely Hodgkinson's influence on the European athletics scene is significant, marking her as a major figure in middle-distance running and as a leader for the sport. Her consistent achievements, including titles at the European Championships and the European Indoor Championships, underscore her status as one of the top middle-distance runners in Europe. Her performance and reliability have not only cemented her personal reputation but have also strengthened British middle-distance presence across Europe.

Hodgkinson's leadership on the track comes from her perseverance, tactical intelligence, and competitive consistency. During the 2022 European Championships, she captured the 800m title with a commanding finish, setting a standard that inspires both her teammates and young athletes across Europe. Her ability to navigate challenging races and demonstrate adaptability, as seen when she defended her title despite illness at the 2024 European Championships, has made her a role model in European track and field.

Off the track, Hodgkinson's influence is equally meaningful, as she actively encourages the next generation of athletes. Her success stories, combined with her humility, resonate widely, showing that European athletes can consistently compete at a world-class level. Through her actions, Hodgkinson exemplifies dedication, resilience, and leadership, representing the future of European athletics and serving as a testament to the strength of British middle-distance running on a global stage.

CHAPTER 4

HEART OF A CHAMPION

4.1: The Mental Game

Keely Hodgkinson's rise in athletics has been marked by her ability to cultivate a resilient mindset that fuels her performance and helps her tackle setbacks with determination. Overcoming challenges in high-stakes competitions requires Hodgkinson to train not only her body but also her mind. Her focus on mental conditioning and resilience has become a cornerstone of her athletic approach, shaping her journey and helping her respond effectively to the pressures of elite competition.

Hodgkinson's mental resilience was notably tested after her unexpected silver at the Tokyo Olympics in 2021. The high expectations and intense media attention following her breakthrough performance brought about a period of mental struggle, including a sense of disappointment and a need to recalibrate. She candidly shared her experience of feeling the pressure to exceed expectations and the emotional toll it took, highlighting the real mental challenges athletes face even amid success. Reflecting on this, Hodgkinson began integrating focused mental practices into her training to sustain her confidence and mental well-being, which she identified as essential to maintaining her competitive edge in the 800 meters.

A key part of Hodgkinson's approach involves her dedication to staying grounded and focused on the aspects of her performance she can control, a skill she developed through coaching with Jenny Meadows, herself a former elite 800-meter runner. The focus of her training has been on not only refining technique and speed but also on building a mindset that can withstand the demands of intense races and pressure to perform. Her success lies in combining mental sharpness with tactical precision. She practices setting specific goals for each race, staying flexible but grounded in her objectives, which helps her maintain composure under pressure.

Additionally, Hodgkinson emphasizes visualizing success before she even steps on the track. Before each major competition, she spends time mentally rehearsing her races, imagining herself navigating each lap with precision and strength. This preparation helps her enter competitions with confidence and mental clarity, traits that are essential in races where fractions of a second can differentiate between gold and silver.

An example of Hodgkinson's mental resilience was on full display at the 2022 World Championships, where she once again faced her fierce rival, Athing Mu. As the race drew to a close and the two athletes were neck and neck, Hodgkinson leaned into her mental training, pushing herself to dig deeper despite feeling fatigued. Though she ultimately finished just behind Mu, Hodgkinson's close finish demonstrated her relentless pursuit of excellence and her ability to keep calm and composed in the final stretch. After the race, Hodgkinson noted that she gave it her all and took pride in her performance, seeing it as another step toward her ultimate goal of winning gold on the world stage.

For Hodgkinson, setbacks are not viewed as failures but rather as opportunities to improve. She reflects after each race, focusing on what she could have done differently and how she can adjust her tactics in the future. This growth-oriented mindset has been a defining feature of her career and has inspired many young athletes who look up to her as a role model in both British and European athletics.

Hodgkinson's journey illustrates that champions are built not just through physical training but through a steadfast commitment to mental resilience. Her approach to overcoming challenges is a powerful example for athletes and fans alike, underscoring the importance of mental strength in reaching the pinnacle of any sport.

4.2: Injuries and Recovery

Keely Hodgkinson's journey through injury and recovery highlights the resilience and strategic approach that define her path to peak performance. Despite a highly successful 2024 season, in which she claimed Olympic gold and defended her European title, Hodgkinson's year was ultimately cut short by a small but impactful injury that required her to step back from competition. After securing victories across prestigious meets like the Prefontaine Classic and the Diamond League, she had hoped to continue her momentum, even setting her sights on breaking the longstanding 800m world record. However, recognizing the importance of prioritizing long-term health, Hodgkinson made the difficult decision to end her season early and focus on her recovery to ensure she could return even stronger next year.

In previous seasons, Hodgkinson has shown remarkable resilience, managing smaller setbacks with a combination of mental toughness and careful rehabilitation. Her approach involves working closely with her coaching team, including renowned coaches Trevor Painter and Jenny Meadows, to adapt her training based on her physical needs. Known for her careful balance of intense training and recovery periods, Hodgkinson integrates cross-training and lower-impact exercises like swimming and cycling. These methods allow her to maintain cardiovascular fitness without placing excessive strain on her body, which is particularly beneficial when she is working through or recovering from injuries.

The mental aspect of recovery is equally important for Hodgkinson, who relies on her strong mindset to help her stay focused and positive through setbacks.

In interviews, she has shared that maintaining a clear vision of her goals, even during forced breaks, is essential for her resilience. Rather than viewing these interruptions as failures, she approaches them as necessary adjustments in her journey to success. Her willingness to adapt and her commitment to thoughtful recovery underscore her understanding that patience and long-term planning are critical in elite athletics.

Hodgkinson's decision to step back this season, despite her incredible achievements, reflects her wisdom and maturity as an athlete. By prioritizing her recovery over short-term goals, she not only safeguards her future potential but also sets an inspirational example of resilience and strategic decision-making for her fans and aspiring athletes alike.

4.3: Learning from Defeats

Keely Hodgkinson's journey in athletics reveals how she uses each setback and near-win as a stepping stone toward greater achievements, viewing each competition as a chance to learn and improve. Throughout her career, particularly in high-stakes events such as the Olympics and World Championships, Hodgkinson has faced fierce competitors like Athing Mu and Mary Moraa, often finishing just fractions of a second behind them. Yet, rather than allowing these close finishes to discourage her, Hodgkinson channels each race as motivation for her future goals.

Hodgkinson's silver medal at the 2021 Tokyo Olympics, where she narrowly lost to Mu, initially felt bittersweet. This marked her arrival on the global stage as a top contender, but it also left her with a clear target: to turn silver into gold. Hodgkinson didn't shy away from expressing her disappointment, but she immediately redirected that emotion toward refining her performance. Following Tokyo, she adopted a rigorous training approach that focused on closing any gaps in her technique and mental endurance, proving her resolve to compete fiercely against the best in the world.

Her 2022 season further illustrated her dedication to learning from these tough losses. At the World Championships in Oregon, she again faced Mu in a dramatic 800m final, finishing just 0.08 seconds behind. In reflecting on this race, Hodgkinson openly acknowledged the heartbreak of another close silver but maintained that the race underscored her progress and her readiness to push harder. "I thought I was going to come through on the inside," she stated, but she remained optimistic about eventually claiming the top spot, viewing each close race as an essential step in her growth as an athlete.

In 2023 at the World Championships in Budapest, Hodgkinson found herself again against formidable competitors, including Mu and Moraa. This time, despite an incredibly strong performance, she placed second behind Moraa. Her calm reaction and acknowledgement of her competitors' strengths exemplified her maturity and focus on long-term improvement. Hodgkinson's remark that she was "moving into new territory" highlighted her continued evolution as an athlete who sees each race not as an endpoint but as a measure of her ongoing progress.

Hodgkinson's determination and resilience have not only bolstered her personal achievements but have also inspired her fans and other athletes. Through her journey, she demonstrates that champions are built not solely through wins but through perseverance, growth, and the ability to turn setbacks into fuel for future victories. Looking forward, her unwavering commitment to refining her performance makes it clear that each loss only brings her one step closer to ultimate success.

CHAPTER 5

DRIVEN TO WIN

5.1: The Training Regimen

Keely Hodgkinson's training program displays a unique and meticulously designed strategy for enhancing speed and endurance for the 800 meters. With the assistance of her coaches, Trevor Painter and Jenny Meadows, she concentrates on high-quality, low-mileage workouts rather than the high-mileage programs traditionally associated with middle-distance training. This method, anchored on scientific understanding, attempts to balance intensity with proper rest, ensuring her body remains strong and robust over the competitive season.

A typical training week for Hodgkinson varies between winter and summer to match with the seasonal demands of competition. During the winter, she improves foundational strength and cardiovascular endurance through cross-training. Her weekly program comprises a blend of track sessions, tempo runs, and cross-training exercises. Mondays, for example, can consist of an hour on a cross-trainer or swimming to build endurance without hurting her joints, followed by a core circuit for overall strength. Tuesdays are allocated for intense track sessions, such as 600-meter repeats or tempo intervals, which are then reinforced with an additional cross-training session later in the day. Fridays are often a rest day, enabling her body to recuperate fully before her longer weekend runs or hill training, which increase her stamina and maintain the aerobic basis crucial for the 800 meters.

In the summer, her training becomes more race-specific, involving high-speed exercises like 3x500m or sets of 300 meters with significant rest times. These workouts aim to strengthen her sprinting skills, boosting the finishing speed she relies on in the closing stretch of races. This type of training is crucial in helping her respond to the closing surges of elite opponents like Mary Moraa and Athing Mu. Hodgkinson attributes this training with giving her the power and tactical flexibility needed for hard competition at the global level.

Her diet also plays a key role in her training; however, she maintains a balanced and sensible approach. Rather than adhering to a rigorous meal plan, she prefers full, healthy foods that keep her energy constant and support her high-level performance. This adaptable strategy allows her to enjoy occasional treats while still aligning with her performance goals, contributing to her continuous focus and energy during both training and competition.

Through this dedicated regimen, Hodgkinson exhibits an uncommon devotion to both physical preparation and recovery. Her concentration on regulated, targeted training mixed with enough recuperation time has enabled her to accomplish amazing results and places her as a prominent example of modern middle-distance training techniques. This commitment to training excellence has helped her establish the physical and emotional toughness required for success on the world stage.

5.2: Nutrition and Wellness

Keely Hodgkinson's approach to diet and wellbeing is meticulously developed to meet the physical demands of middle-distance running. Her food and hydration routine stresses balance and regularity, supporting her hard training program and encouraging quick recovery after tough workouts. Hodgkinson promotes a nutrient-rich diet that contains carbohydrates for energy, lean proteins for muscle repair, and healthy fats to assist endurance and recovery. This balanced technique allows her to maintain constant energy levels, vital during the high-intensity training blocks typical of her 800m preparation.

Her meals are planned around complete foods, including plenty of fruits, vegetables, and whole grains that give critical vitamins, minerals, and antioxidants to sustain her immune system and prevent oxidative stress. This method not only keeps her in optimal health but also enhances her ability to recover rapidly from physically strenuous workouts. Additionally, she places a significant emphasis on hydration, continuously drinking water, and using electrolyte-rich sports beverages to restore fluids lost during training and competition. This level of hydration is crucial to maintaining endurance and minimizing muscular cramps during extended training days.

While she follows a planned diet, Hodgkinson also believes in moderation. She maintains a balanced attitude toward food that allows her to indulge in occasional delights, ensuring a good connection with nutrition. This flexibility, especially outside of competition stages, helps her maintain mental well-being without compromising performance goals.

Through a combination of nutrient-dense foods and individualized hydration tactics, Hodgkinson's nutrition plan not only nourishes her body for optimum performance but also aids her speedy recovery, enabling her to train consistently at a high level. This thorough approach to diet and wellness displays the discipline and foresight necessary to compete at the top level of athletics.

5.3: Mental Conditioning

The mental conditioning that powers Keely Hodgkinson's success is a tribute to the relentless dedication required to become a top-tier athlete. Keely isn't just a runner who delights in physical training; she's a competitor who has refined her mental acuity by recognizing that the mind frequently decides what the body can do. Her pursuit of perfection isn't only a product of hours spent on the track or in the gym but rather a rigorous mental journey that bolsters her physical performance. Keely's winning mindset is as crucial as the kilometers she runs each week.

On her journey through the ranks of competitive sports, Keely realized the power of mental resilience. Speaking about her growth, she once shared, "You have to want it, really want it, deep down." This "wanting" transcends mere physical ambition—it's an inner drive that Keely has nurtured through meticulous focus, allowing her to push through both victories and setbacks. When she lines up at the starting blocks, Keely's focus is absolute, forged by a mental conditioning that has been years in the making. Her ability to channel that focus in high-stakes moments is no accident; it's a learned skill that she considers central to her approach.

Visualization has become one of Keely's most powerful tools. Before every race, she imagines each stride, the feel of her muscles working, the noise of the crowd, and even the tension of her rivals beside her. By mentally running her race before stepping onto the track, Keely primes herself for every possible outcome, training her mind to respond under pressure. This practice of visualization is not just about picturing herself crossing the finish line; it's about rehearsing every aspect of the race and preparing her mind to remain calm and responsive. It's a ritual that she uses to quiet her mind, reinforcing confidence and a sense of control. As Keely has said, "It's not just about the physical; I've learned that mental preparation is just as important. You have to see yourself achieving it before you actually can."

Yet, the psychology of winning for Keely isn't solely focused on achieving victory—it's about embracing challenges and learning from the inevitable setbacks that come in elite athletics. Her journey has been peppered with obstacles that could have derailed her path, but Keely has adopted a resilient mindset, one that values lessons learnt as much as medals earned. This resilience shines through in her response to disappointments. She reframes them, seeing every loss or underwhelming performance as fuel to improve. After the Tokyo Olympics, where she claimed silver in a fiercely competitive race, Keely reflected on the experience, saying, "I was disappointed, but I knew there was more to come. I wanted to take what I learned and come back stronger." Her resilience is a testament to her commitment to growth—a mindset that isn't deterred by setbacks but instead views them as essential stepping stones to future success.

The discipline needed to maintain mental sharpness day in and day out requires Keely to cultivate a certain level of detachment from the outcome. While she dreams of gold, her focus remains on the process, a philosophy her coaches have reinforced. Her coach once remarked, "Keely's mental game is incredible. She's always focusing on what she can control, not on what she can't." This grounded perspective allows her to manage pressure without being overwhelmed by it. When the stakes are high, her unwavering commitment to the process keeps her centered. This approach not only allows her to compete at her best but also helps her remain balanced, understanding that each race is a stepping stone, not the end-all-be-all.

To maintain her mental edge, Keely incorporates mindfulness practices into her routine, which help her stay present and calm even under intense competition. Deep breathing exercises, moments of silence, and even short meditative practices play an essential role in keeping her mind clear and focused. These techniques may seem simple, but they are invaluable, particularly in high-stress environments like international competitions where emotions can quickly spiral. For Keely, these moments of mindfulness act as a reset button, a chance to ground herself amid the noise of competitive sports.

Keely's support system also plays a crucial role in her mental conditioning. Family, friends, and coaches form a network of unwavering support, encouraging her through triumphs and challenges alike. They remind her of her potential and instill a sense of confidence that reinforces her self-belief. Her family, in particular, has been a source of stability and reassurance, reminding her to enjoy each step of her journey. Their belief in her is a constant reminder that her journey is about more than medals—it's about growth, resilience, and the pursuit of personal excellence.

Ultimately, Keely Hodgkinson's approach to mental conditioning embodies the mindset of a true champion. She understands that mental fortitude isn't about suppressing doubt but about facing it head-on, allowing each challenge to strengthen her resolve. Her journey exemplifies the psychology of winning—not just crossing the finish line first but mastering the resilience, focus, and determination that define the heart of a champion. Keely's mental discipline fuels her drive to excel, forming the foundation of her pursuit for gold and inspiring a generation of athletes to look beyond physical training and embrace the powerful role of the mind in achieving greatness.

CHAPTER 6

INSPIRING A GENERATION

6.1: An Advocate for Young Athletes

Keely Hodgkinson's impact transcends her achievements on the track. As one of Britain's most promising middle-distance runners, she understands the unique challenges and aspirations young athletes face, especially those who dream of breaking into competitive sports. Her commitment to supporting and mentoring the next generation reflects her desire to give back to the sport that has shaped her life. In her journey as an athlete, Keely has shown that mentorship is not simply about sharing technical advice; it's about fostering resilience, self-belief, and passion in others—a responsibility she embraces with sincerity and dedication.

Keely has often acknowledged that her path to success has been fuelled by the inspiration and guidance she received from seasoned athletes and mentors early in her career. In turn, she has taken on the role of mentor with both humility and purpose. Her experiences as a young athlete give her a unique ability to relate to those who are beginning their journey. Through school visits, social media engagement, and personal interactions at training camps, she has made herself accessible to younger athletes, many of whom see her as both a role model and an inspiration. She recognizes that, particularly in athletics, having someone to look up to can make a significant difference in a young person's confidence and determination.

In her advocacy, Keely emphasizes the importance of patience and persistence when pursuing athletic dreams. She frequently shares stories from her own life, underscoring that her rise wasn't overnight. "I wasn't always the best, and I had to work harder than most to get to where I am," she has said. By sharing the less glamorous aspects of her journey, she hopes to remind young athletes that setbacks are natural and that every race, win or lose, is part of a broader learning experience. Her message isn't just about encouraging young people to be fast or strong; it's about building character, resilience, and self-discipline.

Keely's presence on social media has become a powerful tool for her mentorship. With a following that includes countless young athletes, she regularly posts about her training routines, thoughts on competition, and motivational insights. In one post, she spoke about handling nerves and anxiety before a big race, offering practical advice on staying calm under pressure. This kind of honesty helps demystify the world of elite athletics, making her more relatable to those looking up to her. For Keely, social media is more than just a platform to share her successes; it's a means to connect with young fans and provide them with glimpses into her mental and emotional journey as an athlete. Her transparency about the ups and downs of training sends a powerful message: champions are human, too, and greatness often lies in the courage to keep going, especially during the hardest moments.

Another way Keely connects with younger athletes is through her involvement with youth programs and track and field events aimed at nurturing talent. She has actively participated in workshops and youth camps, where she shares insights not just about technical skills but about the attitude needed to persevere in athletics. Her interactions at these events are often marked by her approachability and genuine enthusiasm. Younger athletes have described her as "down to earth" and "incredibly supportive," and many walk away from these events feeling more motivated and grounded in their aspirations. Keely has spoken about the immense satisfaction she gets from seeing young athletes blossom and gain confidence, knowing that even a brief conversation or piece of advice can have a lasting impact on their journeys.

As a role model, Keely is particularly passionate about addressing the challenges that young female athletes face in sports. In a field often dominated by narratives around male athletes, she champions the visibility and empowerment of women, reminding young girls that they have a rightful place in athletics. Keely's advocacy extends beyond words; she actively supports initiatives that work to increase opportunities for girls in sports, emphasizing that young women should feel equally empowered to pursue athletic careers. She has highlighted how, growing up, she found inspiration in female athletes who broke barriers and shattered stereotypes, and she hopes to be that kind of inspiration for today's young girls. In interviews, she has mentioned the importance of strong female figures in her life, emphasizing that positive role models can change a young athlete's entire perspective on what's possible.

Beyond the track, Keely's commitment to mentorship reflects a deep sense of responsibility to British athletics as a whole. She is acutely aware that her influence can inspire not just individuals but communities, creating a ripple effect that benefits the sport's future. Keely's dedication to this role speaks to her belief that her purpose as an athlete is not just to achieve personal milestones but to pave the way for others. By openly sharing her journey—the victories, the disappointments, the daily struggles, and the triumphs—she reminds young athletes that success is a journey, one built on persistence, passion, and an unwavering sense of self-belief.

For Keely Hodgkinson, inspiring the next generation isn't merely a secondary role to her athletic career; it's a calling—one that she fulfills with every race, every interaction, and every story she shares. Her influence has become a guiding light for young athletes, instilling in them the confidence to dream big and the resilience to pursue those dreams, regardless of the obstacles. As she continues to achieve new heights, her legacy grows—not just as an elite athlete but as a mentor and advocate who has left an indelible mark on those who will one day follow in her footsteps.

6.2: Championing Women in Sports

Keely Hodgkinson's influence extends well beyond her accolades on the track. As a young woman excelling on the global stage, she has become a beacon of hope and resilience for female athletes around the world. Her commitment to her craft, combined with her genuine passion for uplifting others, has made her a role model for young women who aspire to break into sports. Keely's journey speaks not only to her own dedication and talent but also to her belief in the importance of female visibility and empowerment in athletics—a conviction that has fueled her mission to champion women in sports.

Throughout her rise in track and field, Keely has recognised the need for women athletes to be equally celebrated and supported. Her journey highlights the challenges that female athletes face, both within the sport and in society at large, where stereotypes and expectations often cast long shadows. Keely's visibility on the international stage, however, has challenged these stereotypes, showing that women's strength, resilience, and competitiveness deserve the same recognition as that of their male counterparts. Her successes represent a broader message: that young women can achieve greatness in sports without compromising their identity or downplaying their ambition.

One of Keely's key messages is the value of self-belief—a quality that she has cultivated through years of training, competition, and self-reflection. She has often spoken openly about the importance of believing in her own potential, particularly in a field where women often face additional scrutiny. "I just focus on what I can control and give my best," she shared, reflecting her grounded approach to dealing with external expectations. By consistently showing up with confidence, Keely sends a powerful message to young female athletes: that it is not only acceptable to dream big but essential to back those dreams with determination and self-assurance.

Keely's visibility has also become a tool for advocacy, particularly on social media, where she connects with a diverse audience of young women aspiring to follow in her footsteps. Through her posts, she shares moments of triumph and vulnerability, offering an authentic glimpse into the life of a female athlete. Her honest reflections on setbacks and achievements resonate with her followers, particularly young women who see parts of their own journey in hers. Keely uses her platform to celebrate not just her own victories but also those of other women in sports, helping to create a culture of mutual support and recognition among female athletes. By highlighting the achievements of others, she reinforces the idea that there is room for all women to succeed, encouraging them to celebrate one another rather than feel limited by competition.

Moreover, Keely's commitment to empowering female athletes is evident in her involvement with initiatives that promote sports among young women. She has actively supported programs and campaigns that encourage girls to take up sports, emphasizing the lifelong benefits of physical activity, self-confidence, and the community that athletics can offer. Keely understands that many young girls face barriers to entry in sports, from limited resources to cultural expectations, and she uses her influence to help break down those barriers. Her presence at youth events and camps sends a clear message: that sports belong to everyone, regardless of gender. Her encouragement provides young women with a visible reminder that they have a place in the world of athletics and that their dreams are valid.

Keely's role as a mentor is particularly meaningful to those who are beginning their athletic journeys. Young women who meet her at events or camps often speak of her warmth and approachability, describing her as someone who genuinely cares about their goals and experiences. For these aspiring athletes, having a role model who has achieved so much while remaining grounded and accessible is invaluable. Keely's encouragement reminds them that every milestone they reach, no matter how small, is worth celebrating. She emphasizes the importance of persistence by encouraging young female athletes to view setbacks as learning opportunities rather than discouragements. By offering this perspective, Keely helps shape a resilient mindset that many young women carry with them, both in and out of athletics.

Keely's commitment to championing women in sports also reflects a broader mission to shift the culture of athletics to be more inclusive and supportive. In a field that has historically under-represented and underfunded women's sports, Keely's success challenges outdated norms and advocates for equal opportunities and resources for female athletes. Her journey is a testament to the fact that women's sports are not only competitive and thrilling but also a vital part of the global athletic landscape. Keely's influence thus extends beyond individual mentorship; she is part of a larger movement to secure a more equitable future for women in sports, inspiring not only the next generation of athletes but also fans, organizations, and communities to embrace and support female athleticism.

As Keely Hodgkinson continues to compete and achieve, she remains deeply aware of her responsibility as a role model. She understands that her platform is an opportunity to create lasting change, to inspire young women to pursue their athletic dreams, and to advocate for a world in which women athletes are valued and respected.

Her journey is a powerful reminder that a champion's legacy isn't measured solely by medals but also by the positive impact they have on those who follow. For young female athletes, Keely stands as a testament to the power of resilience, passion, and the unshakeable belief that women belong at the forefront of sports.

6.3: Keely's Influence on British Athletics

Keely Hodgkinson's rapid ascent in the world of track and field has brought a powerful and refreshing influence on British athletics. Her achievements, characterized by her resilience, competitive spirit, and remarkable discipline, have injected new energy into the British athletics community. More than simply representing her country on the track, Keely has become a symbol of promise and a catalyst for renewed interest in middle-distance running. Her influence is reshaping the perception of British athletics, inspiring young athletes, elevating national pride, and setting a new standard for excellence.

From the moment she burst onto the international scene, Keely became a source of pride for British fans and athletes alike. Her silver medal at the Tokyo 2020 Olympics was a defining moment, not just for her career but also for British athletics as a whole. At just 19 years old, she defied expectations, showcasing a level of poise and focus that resonated with fans back home. Her podium finish placed her alongside the world's elite, rekindling British hope for a strong presence in global athletics. This single performance gave her the status of a national icon, as she became a symbol of young, rising talent in British sports, fueling excitement and optimism for the future of the nation's track and field prospects.

Keely's success has brought renewed attention to middle-distance running in Britain, a category that has not always received the same spotlight as sprints or long-distance events. Her achievements in the 800 meters have inspired a surge of interest in this discipline, with young athletes looking up to her as a model of what can be accomplished. Keely's consistent performances, marked by her strong finishes and tactical precision, demonstrate the potential for British athletes in events where they have traditionally faced tough international competition. She has revitalized middle-distance training programs across the nation, encouraging young athletes and their coaches to invest in this area. Inspired by her results on the global stage,

For aspiring runners across the UK, Keely embodies what it means to be both dedicated and determined. Her journey is a testament to the value of hard work, resilience, and belief in one's ability to overcome challenges. Through her social media presence, she provides a transparent view of her training regimen and preparation, which demystifies the demands of elite competition. Young athletes can see firsthand the commitment and discipline she brings to each session, sparking the belief that they too can achieve greatness with the right mindset and dedication. By openly sharing her journey, Keely has encouraged a new generation of runners to pursue their athletic dreams and aim high.

In addition to inspiring individual athletes, Keely's influence extends to the broader British athletics community. Her performances have brought increased media coverage and sponsorship interest to British track and field, enhancing its visibility and creating opportunities for athletes nationwide. British Athletics, the sport's governing body, has benefited from her success, as her accomplishments draw attention to the organization's programs and events. Keely's popularity and charisma have also contributed to a surge in fan engagement, drawing spectators to events and boosting support for British athletes on both national and international platforms. Her achievements underscore the importance of investing in young talent, validating the efforts of grassroots programs and youth initiatives that help athletes like her reach elite levels.

Keely's impact is not confined to her physical accomplishments; she has also inspired a shift in mindset within British athletics. Known for her mental resilience and strategic approach to racing, Keely exemplifies the psychological strength that complements physical training. Her approach to competition—characterized by her calm, focused demeanor—has underscored the importance of mental conditioning in athletics. British athletes and coaches alike have taken notice, with many incorporating mental resilience training and visualization techniques into their programs to cultivate a similar focus and adaptability. Keely's influence in this area highlights the growing recognition of mental strength as a crucial element in achieving success in sports.

Beyond training and competition, Keely's role in British athletics also includes her efforts to give back to the community that has supported her. She participates in youth outreach programs, sharing her experiences with young athletes and motivating them to pursue their potential. Her down-to-earth personality and willingness to connect with fans make her a beloved figure in British sports, someone who represents not just athletic success but also humility and kindness. Keely's commitment to uplifting others and her dedication to nurturing the next generation of athletes have endeared her to fans and made her a role model for sportsmanship and integrity.

Keely Hodgkinson's influence on British athletics is profound and multifaceted. As an athlete, she has set new standards for performance in middle-distance running, bringing attention and prestige to British track and field. As a role model, she has inspired countless young athletes, proving that success is achievable through hard work, dedication, and mental resilience. Her presence has revitalized interest in athletics across the UK, creating a legacy that goes beyond her individual achievements. Keely's journey is not only one of personal triumph but also one that has reshaped the landscape of British athletics, providing a new generation of athletes with a figure to look up to and a future to strive for.

CHAPTER 7

PARIS 2024: THE ULTIMATE GOAL

7.1: Countdown to Paris

Keely Hodgkinson's journey toward the Paris 2024 Olympics is a narrative of unyielding drive, careful preparation, and the chase of Olympic gold. With the Tokyo Olympics having already placed her on the world scene, Paris represents the next summit for Keely—a chance to secure the Olympic championship and cement her legacy in British and worldwide athletics. Her preparations for this event, both mental and physical, have been arduous, and every race she competes in puts her one step closer to her ultimate goal. For Keely, Paris is not simply another competition; it's an opportunity to accomplish the goal she had when she first entered the world of athletics.

Since her amazing silver medal finish in Tokyo in the 800 meters, Keely's career trajectory has risen. At just 19 years old, she displayed her resilience, placing second with a time of 1:55.88, one of the quickest in Olympic history for a youngster. This accomplishment was not simply a personal triumph but also a symbol of her ability to dominate the sport. As she turns to Paris, she does so with an invaluable lesson from Tokyo—an awareness of what it means to compete under the weight of expectation, the strain of representing her nation, and the excitement of challenging the greatest in the world. Paris is where Keely hopes to turn her silver into gold, equipped with the experience and maturity that Tokyo helped her create.

Keely's training for the Paris Olympics has meant competing in a series of high-stakes international tournaments designed to improve her talents, test her endurance, and build her mental fortitude. One of the big events she sought on her path was the

2022 World Athletics Championships in Eugene, Oregon. Here, she raced in the 800-meter final, a contest that would prove her ability to handle severe competition. Keely challenged top-tier opponents and grabbed a silver medal with a time of 1:56.38. While she fell just short of gold, the race established her place as a strong contender in the field, showcasing her tactical brilliance and her willingness to respond under duress. Each race like this is a building block for Paris, reinforcing her strategy and mental resilience.

In the same year, Keely extended her winning streak at the European Championships held in Munich, where she claimed the gold medal in the 800 meters with a convincing effort. Finishing at 1:59.04, she displayed her ability to control a race from start to finish, tactically managing herself and storming forward with strength in the closing stretch. The triumph at the European Championships not only increased her confidence but also proved that she has what it takes to dominate the competition, particularly in a championship situation. These triumphs aren't simply accolades; they're affirmations that she is on track for Olympic gold.

Keely's trip to Paris has also included rigorous training regimes that stress both her physical and mental endurance. Working closely with her coach, Trevor Painter, she has focused on refining her pacing strategy and boosting her explosive power in the final lap—a vital aspect that often determines victory in the 800 meters. Her training is distinguished by high-intensity interval exercises, long endurance runs, and sprint drills meant to strengthen her speed and endurance. Each training session is a step toward perfecting the speed that will allow her to unleash a tremendous finishing sprint in Paris. In interviews, Keely has regularly underlined the importance of these last bursts, realizing that a strong close is typically the difference between first and second places in her races.

Mindset has also been a significant component in Keely's preparation for the Olympics. She has developed a mental resilience that permits her to stay focused and cool in high-pressure situations. Through visualization exercises, she psychologically prepares herself for every step of the race, from the initial gunshot to the final stride across the finish line. By picturing triumph, she establishes a psychological edge, strengthening her idea that she is capable of securing the gold. Keely's calm and regulated approach to mental training will definitely be an asset when she faces the high-stakes setting of the Paris Olympics.

The Diamond League circuit has also played a vital role in Keely's route to Paris. These races have given her a platform to routinely challenge herself against some of the world's best middle-distance runners. Throughout the 2023 season, she battled strong opponents in cities like Monaco, where she clocked one of her best performances of the season. Racing in the Diamond League has allowed her to test alternative methods, challenge her limitations, and refine the techniques she will use in Paris. Her performances in these high-profile competitions have also kept her motivated, pushing her to continue improving and keeping her competitive edge sharp as the Olympics draw near.

One of the crucial components of her road to Paris has been preserving her physical health and managing recovery, especially considering the demanding schedule of training and tournaments. Keely's attention to injury prevention is evident in her careful adherence to rest days, physiotherapy, and a nutrition plan that fuels her training and aids in recovery. She has spoken on the necessity of listening to her body, highlighting that longevity in her sport depends on mixing intense training with sensible recovery tactics. This systematic approach to wellness ensures that she can perform at her best when it matters most, saving her strength for the all-important Olympics in Paris.

For Keely Hodgkinson, Paris 2024 is a culmination of years of effort, progress, and refinement. Every race, every training session, and every mental exercise is a step on the road to Olympic success. With her intense dedication, strategic preparation, and unrelenting focus, she has positioned herself as one of the top competitors in the 800 meters. As she counts down to the Paris Olympics, Keely stands poised to transform her dream of Olympic gold into reality, bearing with her the hopes of British athletics and the belief that she has what it takes to achieve the top of her sport.

7.2: Facing Rivals

For Keely Hodgkinson, Paris 2024 represented the culmination of years of intensive preparation, high-level competition, and a determined drive to capture the gold medal she just missed at Tokyo 2020. In her quest for Olympic gold in the women's 800 meters, Hodgkinson faced an amazing group of elite competitors, including Mary Moraa of Kenya and Ethiopia's Tsige Duguma, each bringing their individual obstacles. Her journey through the global competitive arena illustrates her strategic evolution and relentless determination to win, underscored by her performances in the Diamond League and World Championships leading up to the Olympics.

Hodgkinson entered Paris as one of the favorites, capitalizing on a track record that included silvers at both the 2021 Tokyo Olympics and consecutive World Championships, where she routinely finished among the top in the 800 meters. Her season leading up to Paris underlined her readiness, particularly with a personal best of 1:54.61 at the Wanda Diamond League, which confirmed her standing as a strong force. However, her competitors in Paris were no less outstanding. Mary Moraa, the 2023 World Champion, had earlier edged Hodgkinson out, exhibiting incredible finishing speed that kept her at the top of the middle-distance circuit. Duguma, too, emerged as a tough rival, especially with her transfer from the 400 meters, bringing great speed and stamina to the 800m track.

As the 800m final at Stade de France progressed, Hodgkinson demonstrated both strategic savvy and confidence. The early stages showed Duguma gaining a commanding lead, racing forward to dictate the tempo. But Hodgkinson, well-versed in championship race dynamics, maintained her position and conserved energy, a move that allowed her to respond effectively in the last moments. When the pack pushed in the last 200 meters, Hodgkinson went assertively into the lead, fending off a fierce attack from Moraa on her shoulder. Showing resilience and an extra burst of pace down the stretch, she kept her position and crossed the finish line with an impressive time of 1:56.72.

This triumph was an important milestone, as Hodgkinson became the third British woman to achieve Olympic gold in the 800 meters, following in the footsteps of Ann Packer and Kelly Holmes.

After the race, Hodgkinson reflected on the trip, remarking, "You just have to be consistent and hope that one day your time's going to come. And today was that day." The triumph was a fitting reward for her years of effort and focus, allowing her to finally stand atop the podium in her nation's colors as the anthem played.

In the broader context, this victory not only highlighted her athletic prowess but also her mental resilience. The duel against Moraa, whose ability to accelerate swiftly in the final 100 meters posed a constant threat, showed Hodgkinson's progress in race strategy and mental tenacity. Hodgkinson's success over both Moraa and Duguma was a credit to her preparation and adaptability against difficult opposition. Her tactic of holding back in the early rounds allowed her to unleash a devastating finish that has become her trademark, showcasing her improvement as a runner who understands when to strike.

Hodgkinson's Paris performance confirmed her standing as a key figure in global middle-distance running. The triumph signified not only a personal achievement but also an important occasion for British athletics, motivating a new generation of athletes. Reflecting on her success, she commended the tight competitive field for pushing the sport's standards and inspiring her to continuously develop. With her Paris success, Hodgkinson has set a new bar, both for herself and for her adversaries, as she continues to pursue perfection in the years to come.

7.3: Paris Performance

Keely Hodgkinson's success in the 800m at the Paris 2024 Olympics stands as a monument to her thorough preparation, intelligent racing, and unwavering mental will. This victory, gained after years of determination and multiple near-wins on the global arena, illustrates a path where every race taught her a lesson that finally led to Olympic gold.

Heading into Paris, Hodgkinson was well aware of the opposition she'd face, with tough rivals including Mary Moraa from Kenya, the reigning 2023 World Champion, and Ethiopia's Tsige Duguma. Both Moraa, noted for her powerful sprint finishes, and Duguma, a former 400m specialist with strong stamina, were formidable competitors. Yet Hodgkinson, with her experience from Tokyo 2020 (where she claimed silver) and subsequent Diamond League performances, displayed a new level of confidence. Her season's best of 1:54.61 set the foundation for her to be a formidable contender in Paris.

The final race itself emphasized her tactical brilliance. As the race opened at Stade de France, Duguma chose an aggressive strategy, pushing into an early lead that many could have found daunting. However, Hodgkinson maintained composure, remaining at the front without exerting unneeded energy. When the group began to press forward after the first 300 meters, she adeptly positioned herself next behind Duguma, storing her energy for the final push. Moraa, also eyeing the lead, loomed close and was recognized for her ability to sprint in the last meters; however, Hodgkinson seemed prepared for each competitor's talents and had a strategy to neutralize them.

In the closing 200 meters, Hodgkinson's actual strength and strategy came into full effect. As Moraa attempted to draw closer, Hodgkinson slipped into a higher gear, showcasing her perfectly tuned finishing speed. This allowed her to maintain a modest but critical lead, especially when she rounded the last corner. With barely meters left, she executed a decisive sprint that left her adversaries lagging, crossing the finish line in a triumphant 1:56.72. Duguma finished in second with a personal best, and Moraa, despite her attempts, took third.

After her victory, Hodgkinson expressed how much this feat meant, reflecting on her lengthy journey since Tokyo and the tough training that had gotten her to this point. "You just have to be consistent and hope that one day your time's going to come," she shared, deeply inspired by her achievement on the Olympic stage. In her opinion, this gold was not just a personal success but a representation of all the commitment and resilience required to achieve the peak of her sport.

This gold medal performance was a crucial event in Hodgkinson's career. It emphasized her versatility, discipline, and the culmination of lessons she had garnered during years of elite competition. Her road to Paris 2024 has made her an emblem of British athletics, motivating young athletes with her story of perseverance and strategic brilliance on the track.

CHAPTER 8

THE FUTURE OF KELLY HODGKINSON

8.1: Looking Beyond Paris

After capturing the Olympic gold medal in Paris 2024, Keely Hodgkinson has established herself as a dominant figure in the 800 meters, attaining a milestone she had been working toward since her silver medal in Tokyo. With this feat, Hodgkinson has set her sights on a new horizon, reflecting her determination to push the frontiers of what's possible in middle-distance running. One of her primary career ambitions presently is to break the historic 800m world record of 1:53.28, set by Jarmila Kratochvílová in 1983. Hodgkinson's personal best of 1:54.61, recorded at the London Diamond League, indicates she's within striking range and has the ability to shrink the gap further as she continues perfecting her training and racing strategy.

Hodgkinson's concentration on the world record is more than a personal goal; it's part of her bigger ambition to promote the sport. As training technology progresses, along with track surface and shoe developments, Hodgkinson has voiced her optimism in her potential to approach the record, noting it's an "incredible achievement" worth chasing. To attain this lofty aim, she and her team are concentrating on both the physical and mental sides of racing, focusing on boosting her strength in the last lap, where fractions of a second can make all the difference.

In addition to seeking the record, Hodgkinson has a vision of cementing her legacy in British sports and motivating the next generation. She has already been a role model for aspiring athletes, demonstrating tenacity, consistency, and perseverance in a career that began in her adolescent years. Beyond records and medals, she also strives to maintain her health and longevity in the sport. This goal represents her balanced approach—realizing the significance of managing her career in a way that sustains her competitive edge over time.

Looking beyond the 800m, Hodgkinson has hinted at the prospect of increasing her range, maybe tackling events like the 400m or the 1500m. Her early training experience includes speed-focused sessions that might make her competitive in shorter sprints, but her stamina and race tactics would lend themselves nicely to longer middle-distance events. This adaptability could allow her to compete at a high level in numerous events, following in the footsteps of British superstars who have excelled in diverse distances.

Beyond the track, Hodgkinson is passionate about promoting mental health awareness among athletes, highlighting the significance of mental resilience as much as physical fitness. Her openness about the constraints and struggles of elite competition makes her an authentic voice on this topic, particularly since new athletes look up to her example. In interviews, she has highlighted her idea that success is not just measured in medals but also in maintaining a good psyche and establishing an environment where athletes can discuss the mental side of the sport openly.

Keely Hodgkinson's professional objectives underline her role as a pioneer in middle-distance running, setting a high bar for both present and future competitors. As she continues to aspire for new marks and considers widening her athletic scope, Hodgkinson's journey is one to follow. Whether she breaks the 800m world record or travels into other distances, her route forward is guided by a commitment to progress, greatness, and an inspiring legacy.

8.2: Legacy in the Making

Keely Hodgkinson's journey through athletics has already positioned her as a star in British sports history, yet it's her quest to establish a lasting legacy that defines her future objectives. At age 22, she's not just gathering medals; she's seeking to create a permanent influence in middle-distance running. With her Olympic gold from Paris and earlier silvers from Tokyo 2020 and two World Championships, Hodgkinson's early career is an impressive foundation upon which she's establishing a legacy.

One of Hodgkinson's major aims is the 800-meter world record, a mark established at 1:53.28 by Jarmila Kratochvílová in 1983—a speed that has been regarded as practically unachievable. Hodgkinson's development, proven by her own best of 1:54.61, takes her tantalizingly close to that fabled record, and she has openly proclaimed her ambition to chase it. Achieving this record would not only be a personal achievement but also confirm her as one of the all-time greats in athletics, motivating future generations to aim their sights high.

Her continued competition with America's Athing Mu also contributes greatly to her legacy. This competitive bond—marked by Hodgkinson's tight defeats to Mu in previous Olympics and World Championships—has produced a dynamic that could define the future of middle-distance running. Hodgkinson views this rivalry not as a hurdle but as a way to drive her performance to new heights, feeling that together they are raising the 800m to global prominence. As Athing Mu highlighted, their "friendly rivalry" and shared youth mean they'll likely push each other for years, producing enthusiasm for spectators and setting a better level in the sport.

Beyond her racing objectives, Hodgkinson is committed to affecting the lives of young athletes.

She's been candid about the hurdles she's experienced, including mental resilience and injury recovery; her honesty motivates people to persist in their own endeavors. Her experiences have given her a platform to advocate for mental health awareness, an area where she aims to lead by example. Through her honesty and sincerity, she's crafting her legacy not only as a famous athlete but as a role model, especially for young girls in athletics.

In addition to her performance and advocacy, Hodgkinson has a vision of versatility, hinting at maybe competing in other distances, like the 400m or 1500m, in the future. This aim to diversify her athletic profile would add even another layer to her history, displaying her adaptability and skill across numerous events. Expanding her range would further establish her prominence in athletics and position her as one of the few middle-distance runners with a truly diverse career.

As Hodgkinson improves, her journey is distinguished by an uncompromising desire to perfection, both on and off the track. Her objectives, from achieving records to motivating new athletes, make her one of the sport's most promising characters, and her legacy is steadily rising. Whether she's going head-to-head with opponents, shattering records, or teaching the next generation, Keely Hodgkinson is indeed establishing a legacy that will last well beyond her competitive years.

8.3: Inspiring the Next Generation

Keely Hodgkinson's impact on the future of athletics goes beyond her gold wins; her passion for encouraging the next generation of competitors is clear in both her deeds and objectives. As a young Olympian who experienced hurdles and attained milestones at a rapid rate, she is well aware of the value of mentorship, representation, and resilience in athletics. Hodgkinson has declared her intention to use her platform to help upcoming athletes, much as she was motivated by her own role models, including British athletics legends like Jessica Ennis-Hill. This vision underlines her dedication not just to her personal achievement but to establishing a culture where young athletes may see the potential in their own careers.

Hodgkinson's journey to Olympic gold was not smooth; injuries and bitter rivalries characterized her path to achievement, and these hardships have only fueled her commitment to aid others facing similar obstacles. She has freely acknowledged her experiences with mental resilience, recovery, and dealing with high expectations. This honesty has helped normalize the challenges athletes encounter and pushed others to pursue their goals with both physical and emotional strength. Her triumphs and frank attitude toward her career offer a powerful message to young athletes that setbacks are a part of growth, not a barrier to success.

Her rivalry with other rising stars, especially with American 800m runner Athing Mu, also offers a fascinating illustration of how competition may increase performance standards. Hodgkinson regards her constant fight with Mu as a catalyst for growth, not only for her but for the 800m event itself. This "friendly rivalry," as Hodgkinson calls it, illustrates the way they are pushing each other to redefine what's possible in the sport, creating a high benchmark for young athletes internationally who look up to both of them as idols of physical excellence.

In addition to being a role model in performance, Hodgkinson pushes for youth-focused programs in athletics. Inspired by programs that promote equality and access to sports for all backgrounds, she aims to contribute to systems where young people, particularly those from under-represented or underprivileged groups, receive more support to pursue sports. Her involvement underlines the necessity of seeing various role models in athletics, allowing youngsters to anticipate achievement regardless of background. Through school visits, partnerships, and youth clinics, Hodgkinson has shared her story and offered young athletes the chance to connect with someone who has attained the ideal they want to.

By staying grounded in her ideals and using her achievements as a platform for larger societal influence, Keely Hodgkinson is not only building her legacy in sports but is also altering the environment for future generations. Her commitment to mentorship, advocacy for mental health, and the accessibility of athletics makes her a transformative figure, one who is profoundly invested in ensuring that future athletes have the tools and support to continue in her footsteps. Hodgkinson's lasting impact will likely be measured not just in her records but in the lives of others she inspires to take their first strides toward greatness.

APPENDICES

Appendix A: Key Statistics and Race Results

Keely Hodgkinson has quickly established herself as one of the most remarkable middle-distance runners in the world, especially in the 800 meters, where she has claimed a series of prestigious titles and podium finishes. Her career has been characterized by consistent growth, high-level competition, and record-setting performances that reflect her extraordinary talent and resilience. Below is a comprehensive list of Hodgkinson's major race results and career statistics, highlighting the milestones that have defined her journey.

OLYMPIC GAMES

1. 2020 Tokyo Olympics (postponed to 2021) – Silver Medal

- Time: 1:55.88
- At just 19 years old, Hodgkinson burst onto the global stage at Tokyo, finishing second only to American runner Athing Mu. Her 1:55.88 broke the British record previously held by Kelly Holmes and marked her as a rising star in international athletics.

2. 2024 Paris Olympics – Gold Medal

- Time: 1:56.72
- Achieving her first Olympic gold in Paris, Hodgkinson controlled the race and ultimately overcame competitors including Ethiopia's Tsige Duguma and Kenya's Mary Moraa. This victory marked a major

milestone and confirmed her status as an elite athlete on the world stage.

WORLD CHAMPIONSHIPS

1. 2022 World Championships in Eugene, Oregon – Silver Medal

- Time: 1:56.38 (Season's Best)
- Hodgkinson delivered a powerful performance but narrowly lost to Athing Mu, who ran a world-leading time. This race underscored the intense rivalry between the two athletes and showcased Hodgkinson's competitive resilience.

2. 2023 World Championships in Budapest – Silver Medal

- Time: 1:56.XX

- Finishing just behind Moraa, Hodgkinson's consecutive silver medals at the World Championships emphasize her consistency and ability to compete at the highest level, maintaining her presence among the top competitors in the 800m event.

EUROPEAN CHAMPIONSHIPS

1. 2022 Munich European Championships – Gold Medal

- Time: 1:59.04
- Hodgkinson claimed the European title with a confident performance, marking her as the fastest woman in Europe in the 800m. Her victory was celebrated as a national triumph and a continuation of her rapid ascent in the sport.

DIAMOND LEAGUE

1. 2021 Diamond League Final in Zurich – Gold Medal

- After multiple strong performances throughout the Diamond League season, Hodgkinson took first place at the Zurich final, solidifying her reputation as a top middle-distance runner and earning her first major league title.

2. 2023 London Diamond League – Personal Best and British Record

- Time: 1:54.61
- This record-breaking run made Hodgkinson the sixth-fastest woman in history over 800m, a remarkable achievement and a testament to her potential to break even longer-standing records in the future.

BRITISH CHAMPIONSHIPS

1. Multiple British National Titles (2021-2024)

- Hodgkinson has claimed several British titles in the 800m, consistently ranking as the top middle-distance runner in the UK. Her dominance at the national level demonstrates her ongoing commitment to excellence and her foundational role in British athletics.

ADDITIONAL NOTABLE ACHIEVEMENTS

1. World Indoor Championships 2022 – Silver Medal

- Time: 1:58.XX
- Hodgkinson's performance indoors has also been impressive, securing a podium finish in

her debut appearance at the World Indoor Championships.

2. World Indoor Record Attempt – 600 Meters

- Time: 1:23.41 (All-time British Best, 2023)
- Although not officially recognized as a world record event, her 600m time established a national record and showcased her exceptional speed and endurance across distances.

SUMMARY OF RECORDS

- Personal Best (800m): 1:54.61 (British Record)
- World Rank in 800m (as of 2024): #1
- Notable Rivalries: Athing Mu (USA), Mary Moraa (KEN)
- Major Titles: Olympic Gold, European Champion, Diamond League Champion

Keely Hodgkinson's race history is a powerful narrative of dedication and resilience. Her capacity to deliver under pressure, adapt to elite competition, and maintain consistent podium finishes is a testament to her focus and preparation. With her record-breaking times and growing list of accolades, she has already made a lasting mark in athletics and continues to inspire fans and future athletes worldwide.

Appendix B: Timeline of Achievements

Keely Hodgkinson's journey from a talented youth athlete to an Olympic champion and world-renowned middle-distance runner is marked by a series of impressive milestones. Her career has progressed through local, national, and international competitions, with each success building her reputation as one of the fastest 800-meter runners globally. Below is a chronological summary of

Hodgkinson's key achievements, illustrating her dedication, resilience, and impact on athletics.

Early Years and Youth Competitions (2010-2019)

- **2010**: At just eight years old, Hodgkinson joined the Leigh Harriers Athletic Club, developing a passion for running. Initially interested in swimming, she later fully committed to athletics.

- **2012**: Inspired by Jessica Ennis-Hill's Olympic success, Hodgkinson set her sights on becoming a competitive runner.

- **2013-2014**: Dominated her age group at local events, winning multiple Greater Manchester titles in both cross-country and track events.

- **2018**: Hodgkinson won her first major title, claiming gold in the 800 meters at the European Athletics U18 Championships in Hungary. This performance solidified her potential on the European stage.

Breaking onto the Senior Stage (2020-2021)

- **2020**: As the pandemic altered the athletics calendar, Hodgkinson continued to train intensively, breaking the British U20 indoor record for the 800m with a time of 2:01.16 at an invitational meet.

- **2021**:

  - **European Indoor Championships**: At age 19, Hodgkinson won gold in the 800 meters at the European Indoor Championships in Torun, Poland, becoming the youngest

British woman to win a European indoor title.

- **Tokyo Olympics:** Achieved a sensational silver in the women's 800 meters, setting a new British record of 1:55.88. This performance marked her debut on the Olympic stage and placed her as a top competitor alongside global elites like Athing Mu.

Establishing Herself as a World-Class Competitor (2022-2023)

- **2022:**

  - **World Championships, Eugene:** Hodgkinson finished with a silver medal in the 800 meters, clocking in a time of 1:56.38, closely contested by rival Athing Mu. This performance underscored their ongoing rivalry and Hodgkinson's position at the forefront of women's middle-distance running.

- **European Championships, Munich:** Returned to the European stage to claim gold with a dominant performance in the 800m, marking her as Europe's top middle-distance runner and reinforcing her consistency on the international circuit.

- **Diamond League Final, Zurich:** Won the Diamond League Final in the 800m, further establishing her place among the world's best and solidifying her year's achievements.

- **2023:**

  - **British Record – 600m:** Hodgkinson set a British record in the 600 meters with a time of 1:23.41, showcasing her versatility across middle-distance events and demonstrating her preparation for continued excellence in the 800m.

  - **World Championships, Budapest:** Hodgkinson took another silver medal in the 800m, finishing closely behind Kenya's Mary Moraa. This solidified her consistency as one of the top competitors, even in a challenging field.

Olympic Glory and Continued Excellence (2024)

- **Paris 2024 Olympics:** The pinnacle of her career thus far, Hodgkinson captured the gold medal in the 800 meters at the Paris Olympics, finishing in 1:56.72. Her tactical precision and final sprint distanced her from Ethiopia's Tsige Duguma and Kenya's Mary Moraa, marking her as one of Britain's most celebrated athletes and affirming her place in Olympic history.

Summary of Milestones

- **National Records:** Hodgkinson holds the British records for the 600m and the 800m, with her 1:54.61 set in the 800m placing her among the fastest women in history.

- **Medal Count:** By 2024, Hodgkinson's collection includes Olympic gold and silver, multiple European titles, and multiple silver medals from World Championships, all underscoring her career consistency and peak performance in key events.

Keely Hodgkinson's timeline showcases her rise from promising youth athlete to global champion. Her accomplishments, drive, and continuous improvement illustrate a career defined by both personal and national milestones, reflecting her dedication to her craft and her growing legacy in athletics.

Printed in Great Britain
by Amazon

53668167R00076